Exploring Cultures in the Kitchen

Indian Culture and Cooking

Lindsey Lowe

Cavendish Square

Published in 2024 by Cavendish Square Publishing, LLC
2544 Clinton Street, Buffalo, NY 14224

Portions of this work were originally authored by Tracey Kelly and published as *The Culture and Recipes of India*. All new material this edition authored by Lindsey Lowe.

Website: cavendishsq.com

Children's Publisher: Anne O'Daly
Design Manager: Keith Davis
Picture Manager: Sophie Mortimer

Picture Credits
t=top, c=center, b=bottom, l=left, r=right
Front Cover: Dreamstime: bl, Kumar tr; Shutterstock: DinaDuda br, Rudra Narayan Mitra tl.
Inside: Dreamstime: 17, 19, 43, Doroshenko 7, Eagleflying 38t, Kumar 1r, Nikhil Patil 20-21b, samrat35 23b; iStock: enviromantic 9, Partha Kar 36-37t; Shutterstock: 4, CRS Photo 8b, 38-39b, elhawa 6b, Espies 27b, 33b, 35b, 45, Kelly Gra 5br, HighViews 22t, ImagesofIndia 11Singh Lens 8-9t, Alexander Mazurkevich 10, Don Mammoser 36-37b, Xubayr Mayo 31, R.M. Nunes 5t, Odua Images 41, Andrey Starostin 25b, StockImageFactory.com 28-29t, stockpexel 22b, Storm is me 6t, Mahathir Mohd Yasin 15; Thinkstock: Geoff Goldswain 30-31, Nathan Soumen 1l, 20-21t; Public Domain: Nauzer 30.

Special thanks to Klaus Arras for all other photography.

Cataloging-in-Publication Data

Names: Lowe, Lindsey.
Title: Indian culture and cooking / Lindsey Lowe.
Description: Buffalo, New York: Cavendish Square Publishing, 2024. | Series: Exploring cultures in the kitchen | Includes glossary and index.
Identifiers: ISBN 9781502669018 (pbk.) | ISBN 9781502669025 (library bound) | ISBN 9781502669032 (ebook)
Subjects: LCSH: Cooking, Indic--Juvenile literature. | Food habits--India--Juvenile literature. | Diet--India--Juvenile literature. | India--Social life and customs--Juvenile literature.
Classification: LCC TX724.5.I4 O34 2024 | DDC 641.5954--dc23

CPSIA compliance information: Batch #CSCSQ24: For further information contact Cavendish Square Publishing LLC at 1-877-980-4450.

Printed in the United States of America

Contents

Spotlight on India

India is in southern Asia. It is the seventh largest country in the world. Over a billion people make it the second most populated country on Earth, after China.

India has borders with Bangladesh, Nepal, Pakistan, Afghanistan, Sri Lanka, China, and Bhutan.

cumin

rosemary

bay leaves

chile powder

saffron

peppercorns

Long Live India!

India is a land of contrasts. Around 1.2 billion people live in 29 different states with breathtaking landscapes, from snow-covered mountains to vast green plateaus with lush river valleys. Indian religious tradition is deeply spiritual: Hinduism, Buddhism, Jainism, and Sikhism all started here. Sometimes it is as though India is two nations. In rural areas, people live simply, farming the land as they have done for centuries. In the cities, bustling crowds pack the streets, and many people work for the world's top tech industries. Despite their differences, the people are all joined together in their love of India's colorful, spicy cooking. Jai Hind (long live India)!

Indian cooking is known for its use of spices. Common ones include cumin, rosemary, bay leaf, chile, saffron, and pepper.

The Ganges is a large river in northern India. Hindus believe it is sacred. They bathe in the river and hold religious ceremonies there.

The Taj Mahal in Agra is India's most famous landmark. It was built almost 400 years ago.

Tso Kar is a saltwater lake in Ladakh, in the Himalayas. It is also called the White Lake because of salt deposits on its shores.

Northern India

Much of the vast Himalaya mountain range stretches across the northern part of India. It has some of the highest mountain peaks on Earth, including Kanchenjunga, which is 28,169 feet (8,586 m) high. The Himalayas have the largest snow-covered area outside of Earth's polar regions! Melted water from the glaciers in these mountains feeds India's major rivers—the Ganges, Indus, and Brahmaputra.

Tea plantations turn the hills a lush green color in Munnar, Kerala, in southern India.

South India

The Deccan Plateau makes up most of the southern part of India. This is a huge area of flat lands, or plains. Its altitude (height) goes up to over half a mile (1 km). The plateau has mountain ranges on each side: the Eastern and Western Ghats. The area's hot and humid tropical climate is perfect for growing tea. However, this also makes it prone to fierce tropical storms called cyclones.

The Victoria Memorial in Kolkata was built in 1901–1926 to honor Queen Victoria. It is a reminder of when Britain controlled India.

DID YOU KNOW?

The official language of India is Hindi, but each state has its own official language, too. Some important languages are: Bengali, Gujarati, Hindi, Kashmiri, Kannada, Konkani, Malayalam, Marathi, Assamese, Punjabi, Sanskrit, and Tamil.

The Plains

Millions of Indians live in the broad treeless plains south of the Himalayas. The area is very fertile and good for farming because it gets water from the powerful Ganges River. Much of India's food is grown here—and it takes a lot to feed the country's huge population. However, the area also is hit with heavy rainstorms called monsoons in summer and fall.

Built as a British trading fort in the late 1600s, Kolkata is India's second largest city. It is a major port and industrial center. Wealthy people live in grand houses, but nearby, masses of poor people live in run-down slums. In 1950, Catholic missionary Mother Theresa set up the Missionaries of Charity here to help the poor. It is now a worldwide charity.

Food and Agriculture

More than 60 percent of people in India are involved in food production. Many farmers cannot afford tractors and plows, so the work is done by hand.

Breadbasket

Grains are an important part of the Indian diet. Much of the nation's wheat crops are grown in Punjab, the "breadbasket" of India. The flour is used to make delicious flatbreads called naan, roti, chapati, and paratha. Naan is often flavored with nigella and cumin seeds, and sometimes stuffed with nuts or dried fruit. Wheat is also grown on the plains near the Ganges River, along with rice and corn.

Rice is a very important crop. Grown in the south and the Himalayas, it takes a lot of time and labor to produce. Southern Indians eat it with their meals instead of bread.

Women plant rice seedlings by hand in a rice paddy in Kanchipuram, Tamil Nadu. Rice growing takes a lot of time and effort.

Buffalo and Cows

In rural areas, many farmers keep cattle and buffalo for milk and to make dairy foods, such as yogurt and butter. In fact, India has the largest number of dairy cows in the world—around 45 million! Poor farmers that cannot afford tractors also use cows to pull the plows in the fields. Hindus believe that cows are sacred, so they do not eat their meat.

A woman on a small farm milks a buffalo. Buffalo and cows are kept for their milk and to make dairy products.

Land of Legumes

Legumes are a staple food in India. Many legumes, including different types of lentils, peas, mung beans, pigeon peas, and chickpeas (garbanzo beans) are grown. These foods contain a lot of protein, so they are good for a vegetarian diet, which almost a third of Indian people follow. Legumes are fed to cattle, too. They also enrich the soil they are grown in, making it more fertile for the next crop.

Lentils and other legumes are an important source of food in India. Lentils and beans come in red, brown, green, yellow, and black varieties.

Colorful spices at a market in Goa. Spices give Indian dishes their unique taste.

Putting the Spice into Life

It's hard to think of Indian cuisine without conjuring up the fragrance and taste of spices! Spices have been grown in India for thousands of years. In fact, they were once so valuable that the Portuguese, Dutch, and British took control of India, just so that they could trade them.

Today, India is the world's largest producer of spices. The aromatic flavors of aniseed, cardamom, chile, cinnamon, clove, coriander, cumin, garlic, ginger, nutmeg, saffron, and turmeric make Indian dishes taste special. Garam masala (meaning "hot spices") is a common spice blend. Each family has a secret recipe for it. Spices are used as medicines, too—to help digestion or cure a cold, for example.

Fish Tales

With thousands of miles of coastline and many inland lakes and rivers, it's not surprising that fish and other seafood are an important source of food in India. Many Indian dishes, such as curries and pilafs, are based around fish and shrimp. Fishing is also a major industry, and shrimp is exported (sold and shipped) to other countries in large numbers. Some fisherman have set up cooperatives to share expensive equipment, such as large boats and fishing nets for their catches. They work together in coastal fishing regions, such as the state of Kerala.

DID YOU KNOW?

India is the world's second largest producer of tea, after China. The country grows more than 900,000 tons of tea per year! Tea plants grow well in fairly hot and humid climates, and the northern plains of Assam and Darjeeling produce famous varieties.

Fishermen on the beach in Kovalam, Kerala, sort through the net of fish they have just pulled from the sea.

Let's Cook!

Cooking is a lot of fun! In this book, you will learn about different ingredients, which tastes go together, and basic cooking methods. Some recipes have steps that you'll need help with, so you can ask a parent or another adult. When your delicious meal is ready, serve it up to family and friends!

This tells you how many people the meal will feed.

Serves 4-6

This lists all the ingredients you will need for your meal.

Before you begin, check that you have everything. Get all the ingredients ready before you start cooking.

YOU WILL NEED

* 5 ounces milk chocolate or semisweet chocolate (or half of each)
* 2 large eggs
* 2 tablespoons powdered sugar

WARNING!

When to Get Help

Most cooking involves chopping ingredients and heating them in some way, whether it´s frying, boiling, or baking. Be careful as you cook—and make sure your adult kitchen assistant is around to help!

TOP TIP

You can choose any chocolate you like.

Top Tips give you more information about the recipe or the ingredients.

For many meals, you need to chop an onion. Cut a thin slice off at both ends, then pull off the papery skin. Cut the onion in half down the middle. Put one half, cut side down, on the cutting board. Hold it with one hand and cut slices with the other hand. Hold the slices together, then cut across them to make small cubes. Be careful not to cut yourself!

Some recipes use fresh chiles—and they are very hot! Chile seeds and the white pith makes your skin burn, so always wear rubber or vinyl gloves when chopping chiles. If you don't have any gloves, wash your hands really well afterward, and do not touch your skin or eyes for a while. To chop, trim the chile stalk, then halve lengthwise. Scrape out the seeds and throw them away. Slice the stalk into fine pieces.

METRIC CONVERSIONS

Oven Temperature

°F	°C
275	140
300	150
325	170
350	180
375	190
400	200
425	220
450	230
475	240

Liquid

cups	milliliters
¼	60
½	120
¾	180
1	240

Weight

ounces	grams
1	30
2	60
3	85
4	115
5	140
6	175
7	200
8	225

Sugar

cups	grams
¼	50
½	100
¾	150
1	200

Flour

cups	grams
¼	30
½	60
¾	90
1	120

Garam Masala

Makes 1 jar of spice mix

Every Indian family has their own recipe for mixing spices. Garam means "hot," and masala means "spices." The heat refers to the warmth of the spices.

YOU WILL NEED

* 1 tablespoon cardamom pods
* 1 tablespoon cumin seeds
* 2 tablespoons coriander seeds
* 1 tablespoon peppercorns
* 2 cinnamon sticks
* 1 teaspoon cloves
* 1–2 dried chiles
* ½ teaspoon ground mace

1 Place a skillet on the stove over medium heat.

2 Add the cardamom pods, cumin and coriander seeds, peppercorns, cinnamon sticks, cloves, and chiles to the heated pan.

3 Dry-roast the spices for a few minutes. Using a wooden spoon or a spatula, stir them so they don't burn.

TOP TIP

Garam masala is used to flavor savory Indian dishes. It can be added at the beginning of cooking, or you can sprinkle it in when the dish is almost cooked.

4 Let the spices cool for a few minutes, then crush them with a pestle and mortar. You can also grind them in a spice mill. Stir in the mace.

5 Spoon the garam masala into a clean jar or tin with a tight lid. Keep the spice mix in a cool, dark place, and it will last for several months.

Lentil Dal

Serves 4

Dal is a stew made from legumes, such as lentils. It comes from southern India, where many people are vegetarians (people who don't eat meat).

YOU WILL NEED

* 10 ounces yellow split lentils
* salt and pepper
* 1 bunch scallions
* 1 red and 1 green bell pepper
* 3 garlic cloves
* 3 red chiles
* 2 tablespoons ghee (clarified butter) or cooking oil
* 1 teaspoon each of garam masala (see pages 14–15), turmeric, coriander seeds, and ground cumin

1 In a colander, rinse the lentils with water. Pick out any that are a different color or are empty shells.

DID YOU KNOW?

The word dal means "split pulses," especially lentils. A pulse is the dry seed of a legume. India is the world's biggest consumer of legumes!

2 Put the good lentils in a saucepan, and add 2½ cups of cold water. Add ½ teaspoon salt, and grind in lots of pepper. Bring to a boil. Put the lid on the pan and reduce the heat to low. Simmer for about 25 minutes. The lentils should be cooked, but not too soft.

3 While the lentils cook, wash and trim the vegetables. Slice the scallions into thin rings,and cut the bell peppers into thin strips.

4 Peel and finely chop the garlic. Trim, deseed, and chop the chiles (see page 13).

5 In a wide skillet, heat the ghee or cooking oil. Add the scallion, pepper, garlic, and chiles. Fry for about 2 minutes, stirring all the time.

6 Add the spices, and fry for a few seconds. Spoon in the lentils with their juices. Stir and heat again. Season with salt and pepper, and serve.

RECIPE: Let's Cook!

Chapatis

Makes 12

Many different types of yummy breads are baked in India! There are chapatis, parathas, naans, and rotis. A lot of wheat is grown in the north of India.

YOU WILL NEED

* ¾ pound atta flour
* 1 tablespoon salt
* 1 tablespoon vegetable oil
* 1 cup lukewarm water

1 Put the flour and salt in a bowl and mix. Add the oil, then the water. Knead it to make a smooth dough.

2 Let the dough rest at room temperature for 2 hours.

3 Divide the dough into 12 equal chunks, and shape each into a ball.

4 Flour a work surface, then roll out each ball to make a circle about 4 inches (10 cm) wide.

TOP TIP

Atta is an Indian flour made from hard, stoneground durum wheat. If you can't find it at the grocery store, use wholewheat flour instead.

5 Add a thin dusting of flour to the circles so they don't stick together. Now pile them up on top of each other.

6 Heat a cast-iron skillet. When it's hot, add the dough circles one at a time. Cook for a few seconds on each side. They are cooked when they puff up and show brown spots.

7 When the chapatis are all done, put them in a basket or on a plate. Wrap a clean cloth around them to keep the chapatis warm.

National Celebrations

Indian people celebrate lots of festivals! Some honor gods and goddesses, the changing seasons, or political events. They all involve rituals, singing and dancing, and plenty of delicious foods.

Independence Day

Indian Independence Day is celebrated on August 15. On this day in 1947, the nation gained freedom from British rule after almost 200 years. To show respect, the Indian flag is raised in public places. Children sing songs at school and are given candies. Family and friends gather for lunch or dinner, just as they do on the Fourth of July in the U.S. Kite-flying competitions are also popular. On October 2, India celebrates Gandhi Jayanti, a holiday that honors Mahatma Gandhi. Gandhi was a great political and spiritual leader who helped India gain its freedom. He did this by using nonviolent methods to spread his message. People all around the world were inspired by him. Sadly, he was assassinated (killed) shortly after the new Indian government was set up.

A boy runs through a field with the Indian flag above his head. He is celebrating Indian Independence Day.

This girl has made a *rangoli*—a decoration of patterns using colored sand, rice flour, or flower petals. The design is lit with oil lamps called *diyas*.

Divine Diwali

India's most important holiday is Diwali, the Hindu festival of light. Held for five days in the fall, it celebrates the symbolic victory of light over darkness. Diwali also honors the goddess Lakshmi, who represents prosperity (success). People pray to her to send them good luck for the coming year. In the past, Diwali was celebrated only by Hindu, Sikh, and Jain people. However, the holiday is so enjoyable that today, everyone in the country celebrates!

People clean their homes and give each other gifts to celebrate Diwali. They light candles and diyas to symbolize the triumph of light over darkness. Amazing fireworks are set off into the skies. Indians also prepare large feasts of special dishes. A Diwali dessert called burfi is made from condensed milk and sugar. Sometimes rosewater and almonds are added.

DID YOU KNOW?

Rangoli is a type of folk art that is used during Indian festivals and holidays. Bright designs are made in rice flour, colored sand, or flower petals. They are placed on the floor near the door of homes to welcome visitors—including the goddess Lakshmi!

Sweets made with milk, nuts, and fruits are traditional at Eid al-Fitr.

Eid al-Fitr

About 14 percent of Indians are Muslims, making them the second-largest religious group in India. The most important Muslim celebration is called Eid al-Fitr, which comes at the end of the month of Ramadan. Ramadan is a time when people follow a strict fast to develop self-control. They pray and read the Quran every day. By the end of Ramadan, people are ready for a big feast! The Eid al-Fitr festivities start when the new moon first appears in the sky. Muslims pray together and give money to the poor. Then they dress up, go to local celebrations, and prepare a feast.

A mother and daughter prepare food for a meal to end the month-long Ramadan fast.

Colorful Holi

Holi, or the "Festival of Colors," is a Hindu celebration that marks the arrival of spring. It happens in March, just as green leaves appear on the trees and flowers begin to bloom. People light bonfires and throw chickpeas and popcorn into them. The next day, people come out into the streets, dancing and singing. Crowds of all ages throw colored powders on each other—they try to become as brightly colored as possible to mimic the springtime colors. Some people think Holi began when the young Hindu god, Krishna, threw colored water at some milkmaids as a practical joke. He was a high-spirited god!

DID YOU KNOW?

During festivals, candies are sometimes decorated with edible silver or gold leaf to make them look really special.

The faces of these students are decorated with colored powders to celebrate Holi.

RECIPE: Let's Cook!

Vegetable Curry

Serves 4

This dish is popular during the festival of Diwali. The different vegetables are a symbol of having plenty of food to eat.

YOU WILL NEED

* ⅔ cup dried black-eyed peas, soaked in water overnight
* 1 onion
* 2 garlic cloves
* 1-inch piece fresh ginger
* 1½ pounds vegetables (as many different kinds as possible; for example, baby corncobs, carrots, green beans, cauliflower, tomatoes)
* 3 tablespoons cooking oil
* 1–2 tablespoons garam masala
* about ¼ cup hot water
* salt and pepper
* 2 tablespoons fresh cilantro leaves

1 Rinse the black-eyed peas in plenty of water. Put them into a saucepan and cover with cold water. Bring to a boil, then drain in a colander. Rinse again in cold running water.

2 Put the black-eyed peas back in the saucepan and cover them with water. Bring to a boil again, then turn down the heat, cover, and simmer over low heat for 50 minutes. Check them every 10 minutes. Add a little more water if they start to look dry.

3 Next, peel the onion, garlic, and ginger. Chop the onion and the ginger into little chunks. Crush the garlic. Wash and trim the other vegetables. Now cut the vegetables into bite-size pieces.

4 Put the oil in a deep, wide saucepan, and heat slowly. Add the onion, garlic, and ginger. Fry for a few minutes until they turn golden yellow.

5 Add the vegetables to the pan in small batches, starting with the hardest vegetables. Fry, stirring, for 2 minutes, then add another batch. When all the vegetables have been added, sprinkle with garam masala, then fry for 1 additional minute. Finally, add the hot water and stir.

6 Drain the black-eyed peas and add them to the vegetables. Stir, cover the pan, and simmer over low heat for 15 minutes. Season with salt and pepper. Scatter with cilantro leaves and serve.

TOP TIP

Black-eyed peas are also called cowpeas. They have a lot of protein, so they are a good food for vegetarians.

Seviyan

Serves 6–8

This delicious, sweet dessert is made with milk and seviyan vermicelli noodles. People serve it at the Eid al-Fitr feast at the end of Ramadan.

YOU WILL NEED

* 1 teaspoon green cardamom pods
* 1 tablespoon ghee or coconut oil
* 7 cups milk
* 4 ounces seviyan (thin vermicelli noodles from India or Pakistan)
* 1 tablespoon chopped almonds
* 1 tablespoon finely chopped pistachio nuts
* 2 tablespoons raisins
* ½ cup sugar
* ⅘ cup cream

1 Pop open the cardamom pods. Push out all the green seeds, then carefully chop the seeds with a knife.

DID YOU KNOW?

Ghee is clarified butter made from buffalo or cow milk. It is made by simmering butter until the water evaporates. Grocery stores sell it in the ethnic food section.

2 Put the ghee or oil in a saucepan and heat over low heat. Add the cardamom seeds and fry them for a few seconds. Put the milk in another pan and simmer (don't let it boil!).

3 Break the noodles into smaller pieces, then add to the pan with the ghee and cardamom. Fry them for a few minutes over medium heat. They should turn a light brown color.

4 Add the hot milk, bring to a boil. Turn down the heat, and simmer for 5 minutes. Keep stirring all the time so the milk doesn't burn.

5 Stir in the almonds, pistachios, and raisins. Let everything simmer for about 15 minutes, until the mixture has thickened a little. Keep stirring every few minutes so it doesn't stick to the bottom of the pan.

6 Take the saucepan off the heat. Stir in the sugar and cream. Decorate with some extra nuts. The seviyan thickens as it cools, and you can serve it hot or cold.

Family Celebrations

Family life is important in India. Birthdays and other milestone life events are often celebrated with the entire family. Indian weddings, especially, are usually lavish celebrations!

Happy Birthdays

Birthdays are huge celebrations in India, bigger than Christmas! Hindu children go to school on their birthday dressed from head to foot in a brand-new outfit. They wear bright, colorful new clothes, new shoes, and new accessories, such as bracelets and hair ribbons. At school, children bring candies to hand out to classmates and teachers. Everyone sings "Happy Birthday" to the child on their special day.

At home, a blessing is given to the birthday boy or girl. The whole family gathers to share a large meal at dinnertime. This will include the birthday person's favorite main as well as many side dishes. A big birthday cake is shared. Later, after the guests leave, the birthday person opens their gifts.

Helped by her mother, a small child cuts into a huge birthday cake as the family looks on. Birthdays are a time of joy and family celebration in India.

A young girl ties a braided *rakhi* bracelet on her brother's wrist as a token of sisterly love during a Raksha Bandhan celebration.

Raksha Bandhan

A Hindu festival called Raksha Bandhan takes place in August. This is the celebration of the love and care shared between a girl and her brother or male cousin. It can also be between a girl and someone she considers her brother, such as a family friend.

The sister and brother gather with the family, and she paints a *tilak* on his forehead. She then ties a rakhi around his wrist as a symbol of her love and prayers for his happiness. Then she places a candy in his mouth. In return, the brother promises that he will always protect his sister and gives her his blessing. He gives her a gift of money or jewelry, too.

DID YOU KNOW?

A tilak is a mark painted on someone's forehead with a special powder. It is often a dot or line, but it can be other shapes, too. It is worn by some Hindus as a religious symbol. On a woman, a type of tilak called a bindi can indicate that she is married.

Samskara Rituals

A samskara is a ritual that marks an important day or event in a person's life. For children, two important samskaras are ones that are performed on the day they start school and the day they graduate. Marriage is another important samskara. The last samskara of life is a ritual performed when a person dies.

A couple celebrates the *annaprashana* samskara, which marks their baby's first taste of solid food.

An Indian couple prays at their traditional wedding ceremony. The bride wears a bright pink and red sari.

Wedding Samskara

Marriage is an important step in a person's life. In India, parents sometimes choose a life partner for their son or daughter. This is called an arranged marriage. People believe that not only do the bride and groom marry, but their families do, too. The wedding lasts several days so the families can get to know each other at festive meals and parties.

There are many marriage customs. Before the wedding, the bride is decorated with *mehndi*, or beautiful henna patterns. The groom often rides to the ceremony on a white horse. The couple then puts floral garlands on each other to show their love. Under a *mandap*, or canopy, they say their marriage vows with a priest around a sacred fire.

This bride has temporary henna tattoos on her hands.

DID YOU KNOW?

The wedding mehndi custom goes back 5,000 years. It became fashionable with non-Indians in the late 1990s. Stars such as Beyoncé have worn mehndi tattoos. Modern versions even use glitter!

RECIPE: Let's Cook!

Tandoori Chicken

Serves 4

Traditionally, this spicy Indian chicken dish is cooked over charcoal in a clay oven called a tandoor. The dish is a favorite at family celebrations.

YOU WILL NEED

* 2 garlic cloves
* 2-inch piece fresh ginger
* 4 teaspoons tandoori spice mix
* ½ cup low-fat yogurt
* 4 chicken thighs
* 2 whole chicken breasts with bones
* olive oil for brushing
* salt

TO SERVE

* lettuce
* juice of 1 lemon
* 2 teaspoons ground cumin
* 2 onions, cut into slices
* fresh mint leaves, to garnish
* yogurt dip

1 Peel the garlic and ginger. Chop finely and put into a big bowl. Add the tandoori spices and yogurt, and stir well to mix.

2 Add the chicken thighs and breasts to the bowl. Brush the pieces with the yogurt mix, then cover the bowl. Chill in the refrigerator overnight or for 12 hours.

SAFETY TIP

Always wash your hands with soap and warm water after handling raw chicken. Use different cutting boards and utensils for raw meat and produce.

3 Preheat the oven to 450°F. One by one, take the chicken pieces out of the yogurt sauce and pat them dry with paper towels. Place them on an oven rack and bake for 20 minutes.

4 Using tongs, turn each chicken piece over. Brush them with a little oil and sprinkle with salt. Bake for another 20 minutes.

5 Put lettuce leaves on a platter. Add the cooked chicken. Drizzle with lemon juice and sprinkle with cumin. Add onion slices, and garnish with mint leaves. Serve with yogurt dip.

DID YOU KNOW?

The spices that go into tandoori seasoning include ginger, nutmeg, paprika, cardamom, cinnamon, cloves, coriander, cumin, turmeric, and pepper.

Vegetable Samosas

Makes 16–20

Most people like samosas. They are a tasty, healthy snack or appetizer! They are delicious eaten warm and dipped in fruit chutney or a spicy dip.

YOU WILL NEED

FOR THE PASTRY

* 3½ tablespoons ghee or oil
* 2 cups all-purpose flour
* 1 teaspoon salt
* 1 teaspoon lemon juice

FOR THE FILLING

* 7 ounces potatoes
* ¼ cauliflower
* 1 small zucchini
* 2 tablespoons ghee or vegetable oil, plus extra for frying the samosas
* 2 teaspoons garam masala
* 1 teaspoon ground ginger
* ½ teaspoon turmeric
* 1 teaspoon cayenne
* ½ teaspoon ground cumin
* salt

1 Melt the ghee in a saucepan over low heat. Put the flour, ½ cup lukewarm water, salt, and lemon juice in a bowl and add the melted ghee. To make a smooth dough, knead for about 10 minutes. Wrap the dough in plastic wrap to keep it moist, then let it rest for 30 minutes.

2 To make the filling, peel the potatoes and cut into cubes. Wash, trim, and chop the cauliflower and zucchini. Heat the ghee or oil in a saucepan. Add the vegetables and fry, stirring, for 2 minutes. Add the spices and salt. Fry and stir for 1 minute. Pour in ½ cup water and cover the pan. Turn down the heat and simmer for 10 minutes. Remove the lid and simmer until the liquid is gone.

DID YOU KNOW?

Samosas can be filled with other vegetables. In India, they often have a potato and pea filling with cashews.

3 Knead the dough once more, then roll it out in small sheets. Put a plate 8 inches (20 cm) in diameter on top of the dough. Cut a circle around it. Knead the leftover dough pieces, then roll them out again and cut more circles.

4 Cut each dough circle in half and put 1 heaped teaspoon of filling in the middle of each. Wet the edges with a little water. Now fold one corner over on top of the other, and squeeze the straight and the round edges together to form the samosa.

5 In a skillet, heat the remaining ghee or oil. Fry the samosas, a few at a time, for about 2 minutes. Turn carefully and fry for 2 more minutes. Lift them out onto paper towels using a slotted spoon. Serve with onion slices and dips.

Life in India

About one-third of the population of India live in its huge, sprawling cities. Most of the people still live very simply in rural villages.

City Life

India's major cities are teeming with millions of people. Wealthy homes stand just down the street from run-down slums, where people live in extreme poverty. In Mumbai, cars, textiles, and machinery are manufactured, employing lots of people. Delhi, India's capital, is a major business center. Many young people here work in jobs at call centers for companies in other countries. Kolkata is a big industrial city and port, but it is also home to thousands of street children.

People walk through Chawri Bazar, a busy market that sells metal and paper products. Delhi is a crowded city of around 15 million people.

People buy vegetables and fruit at simple local markets. These markets are common all across India.

Rural Life

Around two-thirds of Indian people live in small villages in the countryside. Families farm small plots of land to grow food for themselves. Most of it is done by hand, so the work is hard. Sometimes children cannot go to school because they are needed to help grow and harvest crops. Any extra food is sold in the local markets.

Some villages have electricity, but many still don't have running water. Women walk to wells and carry water home in buckets. They wash clothes in rivers and streams. Where there are no sewage facilities, diseases can spread easily as human waste gets into the ground and rivers.

DID YOU KNOW?

Indian Railways runs one of the biggest and busiest railroad networks in the world. It employs 1.3 million people, making it one of the largest employers in the world, too.

DID YOU KNOW?

More movies are made in India than anywhere else in the world. Bollywood is part of the movie industry based in Mumbai (Bombay). The name takes the "B" from "Bombay" and the rest from "Hollywood."

Going to School

In India, children between the ages of 6 and 14 can attend state schools for free. First, they go to lower primary (ages 6 to 10) and upper primary school (ages 10 to 14). They then attend high school (ages 14 to 18), which is split into secondary and higher secondary school.

Private schools with low-cost tuition have become popular in India. Many poor families scrape together the money to send their children to them, because children will receive a better education there. If children are well-educated, they have a chance of finding better jobs and escaping poverty. Students study hard to get good grades!

Many families cannot afford enough food. These schoolchildren have been given a free lunch.

Time Out

Bollywood movies are a popular way for people to relax after work or school. They are full of adventure, romance, singing, and dancing. People also listen to music, such as Indian classical or *bhangra*, which mixes Punjabi folk with Western pop music. Sports are very popular, too, especially cricket. Indians follow their favorite teams and play the game themselves when they have free time.

This Bollywood actress wears bright, colorful clothes. Bollywood movies feature lots of dancing and singing!

A thali tray contains a selection of rice, curries, chutneys, and breads, made to be eaten using the hands.

Family Matters

Extended families often live together in India. This means parents, siblings, grandparents, uncles, aunts, and cousins may all share one home! This is easier in the country, where houses have more room. In cities, homes are smaller, and it's not always possible to live in one place.

Meals offer families a chance to spend quality time together. Delicious foods made with fragrant spices are always prepared fresh. Popular dishes include lentil dal or a thali, a tray with rice, chapatis, chutney, and a vegetable curry or rogan josh.

Cooling Lassi

Makes 6–8 glasses

This chilled yogurt drink is just the thing on a summer day! It also helps cool your mouth if you are eating hot, spicy food.

YOU WILL NEED

* 1 cup whole-milk yogurt
* 1 cup chilled water
* salt
* ½ teaspoon ground cumin
* 1 teaspoon lemon juice
* crushed ice
* some fresh mint leaves

1 Put the yogurt, chilled water, salt, ground cumin, and lemon juice into a large cup or bowl.

2 Mix all the ingredients with a spoon or a whisk to combine. Stir them well to make a smooth, icy drink.

TOP TIP

Use an ice crusher to crush the ice cubes. If you don't have one, put the cubes in a plastic bag, wrap it in a towel, and pound with a rolling pin.

3 Half-fill the glasses with crushed ice, then pour the lassi on top. Decorate the drinks with fresh mint leaves and serve.

TOP TIP

Mango lassis are easy to make. Mash the flesh of 1 mango with 4 cups whole-milk yogurt, 1 cup chilled water, and 4 tablespoons sugar. Put crushed ice into glasses and add the lassi.

RECIPE: Let's Cook!

Rogan Josh

Serves 4

This dish is a classic North Indian favorite. It tastes great served with basmati rice. Every family has their own "secret" recipe!

YOU WILL NEED

* 2 pounds lamb (from the leg)
* ½-inch piece ginger
* 3 garlic cloves
* 2 onions
* 5 tablespoons ghee or oil
* ½ cup whole-milk yogurt
* salt
* fresh cilantro leaves

FOR THE SPICE MIXTURE

* ½ teaspoon ground cardamom
* a pinch of ground cloves
* ½ teaspoon ground black pepper
* a pinch of ground cinnamon
* 1 teaspoon hot paprika
* 1 teaspoon ground coriander
* 1 teaspoon ground cumin

1 Using a clean cutting board and a sharp knife, cut the lamb into bite-size chunks.

DID YOU KNOW?

Rogan josh is traditionally made with mutton, a meat that comes from an older sheep than lamb. It has a stronger flavor and needs to be stewed for a long time.

2 Peel the ginger, garlic, and onions, and chop them into small pieces. Mix the spice mixture in a small bowl.

3 Put the ghee or oil in a large saucepan and heat. Add the meat chunks and fry them, stirring, until they are browned all over and no longer look pink.

4 Remove the meat and set it aside. Now add the garlic, onions, and ginger. Fry for 2 minutes. Add the spice mixture, stir, and fry for 2 more minutes.

5 Put the meat back in the saucepan. Add the yogurt, 1 cup water, and 1 teaspoon salt, and stir. Simmer for 1 hour over low heat.

6 Every 10 minutes or so, stir the mixture, adding more water if it gets too dry. Scatter fresh cilantro on top when done and serve with cooked basmati rice.

Coconut Pilaf

Serves 4

This fragrant, flavorful recipe from Kerala is often made as a vegetarian dish. Here, shrimp is added. Coconut milk brings the flavors together.

YOU WILL NEED

* 2 cups basmati rice
* salt
* 4 garlic cloves
* 2-inch piece fresh ginger
* 1–2 chiles
* 2 teaspoons ground cumin
* 1 teaspoon ground cardamom
* a pinch of ground cinnamon
* 1 large onion
* 2 tablespoons cooking oil
* 3 tomatoes
* ½ cup full-fat yogurt
* ½ cup unsweetened coconut milk
* ¾ pound peeled cooked shrimp (or cubed chicken)
* 2 tablespoons cashews, chopped and roasted
* a handful of scallion slices

1 Rinse the rice in a colander. Put it in a saucepan with 2½ cups of cold water and 1 teaspoon salt. Bring to a boil, stir, and cover. Simmer the rice over low heat for 15–20 minutes. If it looks dry, add a little more water.

2 Next, peel the garlic and ginger. Trim and deseed the chiles (see page 13). Put garlic, ginger, chiles, cumin, cardamom, and cinnamon into a cup with 3 tablespoons water. Use an immersion blender or hand mixer until it becomes a fairly smooth paste.

3 Peel and chop the onion. In a deep skillet, heat the oil, add the onion, and fry until it is golden brown. Chop the tomatoes.

4 Add the spice paste and stir well. Using a wooden spoon, stir in the tomatoes, yogurt, and coconut milk. Cook over medium heat for 10 minutes, stirring from time to time. Add the shrimp and cook for another 3–4 minutes.

5 Add in the rice and season with a little salt. Scatter the roasted cashews and scallions across the top of the dish and serve.

DID YOU KNOW?

"Pilaf" is originally a Persian word. There are different spellings, such as pilau, pilav, pulao. The main ingredient in pilaf is usually seafood or chicken. Nuts, coconut, and dried fruits are often added as well.

Glossary

agriculture Another word for farming; the growing and harvesting of crops and the raising of animals.

chapati One of many different types of bread in India.

chutney A condiment made from fruits or vegetables, spices, vinegar, and sugar.

dal (1) A legume; a dried split bean or pea; (2) a stewlike dish made from legumes.

Diwali The Hindu Festival of Lights, one of the biggest Indian celebrations.

garam masala A spice mix that is often sprinkled on a dish at the end of cooking.

ghee Clarified butter used in Indian cooking.

henna The powdered leaves of a shrub used to make mehndi (a temporary tattoo) or hair dye.

Holi A festival marking springtime where people throw colored powders and paints on each other.

lassi A drink made with yogurt or buttermilk.

legumes A plant that is a member of the pea family, including beans and lentils. The dried seeds of a legume are called pulses.

mehndi (1) A temporary tattoo applied to the hands and feet, especially before a wedding; (2) the party at which wedding tattoos are applied.

samosa A deep-fried pastry triangle filled with vegetables or meat.

samskara A life-cycle celebration, such as a birth, name-giving, first day of school, or a wedding.

seviyan A sweet dessert dish eaten or given for the Muslim festival of Eid al-Fitr.

tandoor A clay oven that reaches a high temperature and is used for cooking dishes such as tandoori chicken and breads.

tandoori spice mix A reddish-yellow spice mixture applied to chicken or other dishes before cooking in the tandoor.

thali A silver tray used to hold several different Indian dishes, such as curries and dals, chutneys, rice, and pieces of bread.

Further Resources

Books

Bilan, Jasbinder.
India, Incredible India.
Walker Books, 2022.

Chawla, Penny.
50 Easy Indian Curries.
Smith Street Books, 2022.

Deshmukh, Nia.
Summarized Indian Cookbook for Kids.
Independently published, 2022.

Doeden, Matt.
Travel to India.
Lerner Publishing, 2022.

DK Authors.
Timelines from Indian History.
DK Children, 2022.

Walker, Cindy.
Indian Holiday Foods (Holiday Around the World).
Independently published, 2022.

Websites

www.kids-cooking-activities.com/Indian-cooking.html
Pages with facts, recipes, and video links about India.
www.kids-world-travel-guide.com/india-for-kids.html
General information about India, its history, customs, and food.
www.rainforestcruises.com/guides/india-food
Pages showing large photographs of the 25 most popular traditional dishes to eat in India.
www.rainforestcruises.com/guides/indian-festivals
Pages explaining the festivals and celebrations of India.

Publisher's note to educators and parents: Our editors have carefully reviewed these websites to ensure that they are suitable for students. Many websites change frequently, however, and we cannot guarantee that a site's future contents will continue to meet our high standards of quality and educational value. Be advised that students should be closely supervised whenever they access the Internet.

Index